Night
Rescue

by Benjamin Hulme-Cross
Illustrated by Bill Ledger

OXFORD
UNIVERSITY PRESS

In this story ...

Jin
(Swoop)

Jin has the power to fly. He once had a race with a jumbo jet ... and won! He can even fly high enough to reach outer space!

Cam
(Switch)

The Head
(head teacher)

Chapter 1:
Night race

Jin and Cam had been practising their hero skills outside, and now they were racing back to the academy for dinner.

"Keep up, slowcoach!" said Jin, as he raced ahead of Cam.

Cam flapped her bat-wings harder and caught up with Jin. They zoomed over the sports pitch.

Just then, Jin spotted something through his night-vision goggles. It was hopping along the ground below, away from the academy, carrying something shiny in its paws.

"Cam! There's a bunny-wunny!" Jin yelled.

Bunny-wunnies meant only one thing ... trouble!

Bunny-wunnies

Bunny-wunnies are robotic rabbits. They were invented by Ray Ranter to help him with his dastardly plans. Ray Ranter is an enemy of Hero Academy.

paws which can turn into saws, umbrellas and other tools

front pouch

Jin landed, skidding to a halt outside the front door of the academy. Cam flapped down next to him and changed back into a girl.

"What was that bunny-wunny doing?" Cam said.

"I don't know," Jin replied, "but we need to raise the alarm."

The two heroes raced inside.

Chapter 2:
Where is everyone?

"Don't worry," said Jin, as they rushed towards the staffroom. "The teachers will sort this out."

However, when they arrived at the staffroom, it was empty.

"Where are they?" Cam asked.

"The Head will know," Jin replied, hurrying on.

When they got to the Head's office, they found him shouting instructions into a screen.

"... Ranter Tower," the Head was saying. "Take him to the basement."

Jin didn't wait to hear more. "There's a bunny-wunny outside!" he told the Head.

The Head looked at him, narrowing his eyes. "Don't be ridiculous," he said.

Jin's mouth dropped open in surprise. The Head wasn't normally so rude.

"Where are the teachers?" Cam asked.

"Oh, I told them to go out for the evening," the Head replied.

"But the bunny—" Before Jin could finish, the lights cut out.

"Now what?" complained the hologram. "Who would have thought that being the Head would mean so much work?"

Jin pulled on his night-vision goggles and gasped in shock. With the goggles on, Jin could see that the hologram wasn't the Head at all – it was Ray Ranter in disguise!

Chapter 3:
Ranter Tower

Jin and Cam raced to the roof of the academy. Jin had been shocked to see Ranter, and he knew they had to get to a place where they wouldn't be overheard.

"Why don't you stay here and keep an eye on Ranter," said Jin. "I'll go to Ranter Tower. He must have taken the real Head there. He was talking about the basement."

Before Cam could object, Jin spun into his
super suit and became Swoop. Then he put his
goggles back on, sprinted across the rooftop
and leaped into the night sky. The air whooshed
across his body, and he squeezed his eyes shut.

"If only I wasn't afraid of heights," he thought
for the millionth time.

When Swoop opened his eyes, the city lights twinkled below him like multi-coloured stars. He could see Ranter Tower in the distance.

In less than a minute, he landed in an empty street behind the tower.

Swoop ran down some steps and rattled the handle on the basement door. There was a screen, low down on the wall next to the door, which flashed a message: EYE SCAN: LOOK DIRECTLY AT THE SCREEN.

Swoop was about to turn away when he heard a snuffling sound. A bunny-wunny popped through a small flap in the door.

Swoop grabbed the bunny-wunny and held it up so that its eye was in front of the security screen.

A blue light scanned the bunny-wunny's eye, and a new message flashed up on the screen: YOU MAY ENTER.

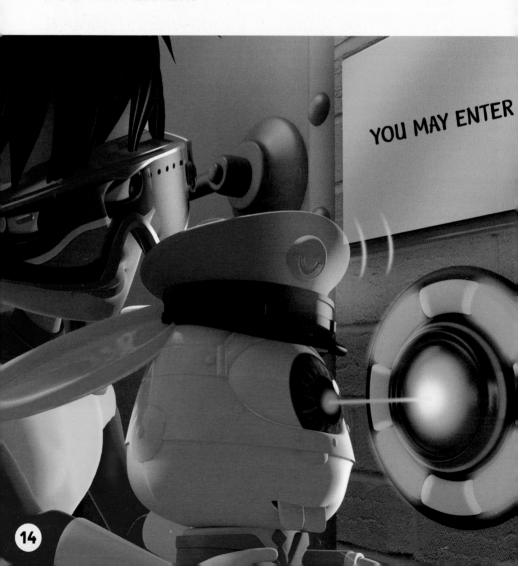

"Thanks, little fella," said Swoop, dropping the furious bunny-wunny into a nearby rubbish bin. "That was easier than I thought," he muttered, as he pushed the door open and entered Ranter Tower.

Chapter 4:
Time to play!

The basement looked like a big, dark underground car park. As Swoop took a step inside, however, the lights turned on. He took off his night-vision goggles and gasped. The room was full of Ranter's bunny-wunnies. In the middle of them was a table, and on the table was …

"The Head's holo-projector!" Swoop said.

The bunny-wunnies all turned to face the intruder. Swoop froze.

"There must be over a hundred of them," he thought. Swoop wished Cam was with him. "Calm down," he told himself. "It's not as if they can fly." He floated up until he was hovering out of reach, above the bunny-wunnies' ears.

The bunny-wunnies stared up at Swoop as he flew towards the table. One of them jumped up, trying to grab him.

"Whoa!" Swoop shouted, swerving out of the way.

Then, the bunny-wunnies began jumping on top of each other to form stacks. Swoop was forced higher into the air ... too high to reach the holo-projector.

Just then, a small, black shape flitted past. Swoop glanced up. It was a bat, and it was heading straight towards the holo-projector.

"Cam!" he thought.

Swoop knew he had to keep the bunny-wunnies focused on him, so they would not see Cam.

"Time to play!" Swoop shouted, zooming down towards the bunny-wunnies. They jumped up at him again, but Swoop remained just out of reach.

Out of the corner of his eye, Swoop saw Cam turn into Switch by the table. She snatched up the holo-projector.

"Over here, you pesky rabbits," Swoop cried, and the bunny-wunnies followed him away from the table.

Switch sprinted for the exit. The bunny-wunnies heard her. They turned at once and began bouncing after her.

They were too late! Switch had made it to the door. Swoop shot over their heads, following Switch outside.

"Great job, Switch!" Swoop said. He took the holo-projector from her.

A moment later, Switch turned back into a bat. She and Swoop flew away.

Chapter 5:
Dealing with Ranter

Back at the academy, Swoop and Switch strode into the Head's office and set the holo-projector down next to Ranter's fake projector.

The real Head looked furious.

"RANTER!" he yelled. "The game's up."

"Uh, oh!" Ranter said.

"I'm shutting you down and taking back control of Hero Academy," the Head said.

Immediately, Ranter's hologram began to fade out.

"I'll ... be ... back ..." Ranter raged, his voice breaking up.

"Bye, bye," laughed Switch, as the hologram disappeared.

"Well done, Swoop and Switch," said the real Head. "Your bravery has saved Hero Academy!"

Through the window, the heroes could see several teachers chasing a group of bunny-wunnies away.

Swoop turned to Switch. "We've just got time for another flying race before dinner."

Switch's fingers tingled as she began to shape-shift. "You're on!"